SENT...

STUDY GUIDE

ISBN: 978-1-960678-53-9   1 2 3 4 5 6 7 8 9 10

Printed in the United States of America

STUDY GUIDE

SENT...

THE AMAZING CONNECTION BETWEEN
OUR DESTINY AND THE GUIDING PRINCIPLE
OF THE LIFE OF CHRIST!

MÄRT VÄHI

CONTENTS

SENT...

THE AMAZING CONNECTION BETWEEN
OUR DESTINY AND THE GUIDING PRINCIPLE
OF THE LIFE OF CHRIST!

MÄRT VÄHI

WHOSE WAY?

Could it be that the "Me" generation has, to some degree, always existed and always will?

REVIEW, REFLECT, AND RESPOND

READING TIME

As you read
Chapter 1:
"Whose Way?"
in *Sent...*
review, reflect
on, and respond
to the text by
answering
the following
questions.

How would you define the "Me" generation in your own words?

_____

_____

_____

_____

_____

_____

_____

_____

_____

How do the principles of the "Me" generation go against Jesus's life and ministry?

_____

_____

_____

_____

_____

_____

_____

_____

_____

Now large crowds were going along with Him, and He turned and said to them, "If anyone comes to Me and does not hate his own father, mother, wife, children, brothers, sisters, yes, and even his own life, he cannot be My disciple. Whoever does not carry his own cross and come after Me cannot be My disciple.

—Luke 14:25-27

Consider the scripture above and answer the following questions:

What is the meaning of this verse? What stands out to you?

_____

_____

_____

_____

_____

_____

Do you think Jesus actually means to hate our father, mother, wife, etc.? Why or why not?

_____

_____

_____

_____

_____

_____

Do you ever struggle with this level of commitment?

_____

_____

_____

Have you ever chosen your way instead of God's way? Describe the situation.

_____

_____

_____

_____

_____

Are you willing to go God's way, even if it entails sacrifice, hardships, and uncertainty? Why?

_____

_____

_____

_____

_____

How can you discern God's way from your own?

_____

_____

_____

_____

_____

YOU WERE BORN FOR AND WITH A PURPOSE!

There is a destiny that exists for you independent of circumstances, situations, opinions, or any set of conditions which may seem to be ruling your life right now.

As you read Chapter 2: "You Were Born for and With a Purpose!" in *Sent... review, reflect on, and respond to the text by answering the following questions.

REVIEW, REFLECT, AND RESPOND

What was Christ's purpose? Do you believe you have a purpose, just like Jesus Christ?

_____

_____

_____

_____

_____

What do you think can stop you from achieving your divine purpose? Explain your answer.

_____

_____

_____

_____

_____

_____

What has God brought you through to get you to where you are today? Did you realize what He was doing at the moment—or only after the fact?

_____

_____

_____

_____

_____

_____

> *I will stand on my guard post and station myself on the watchtower; and I will keep watch to see what He will say to me, And how I may reply when I am reprimanded. Then the LORD answered me and said, "Write down the vision and inscribe it clearly on tablets, So that one who reads it may run. For the vision is yet for the appointed time; It hurries toward the goal and it will not fail. Though it delays, wait for it; For it will certainly come, it will not delay long.*
>
> *—Habakkuk 2:1-3*

Consider the scripture above and answer the following questions:

What is the meaning of this passage?

_____

_____

_____

_____

_____

_____

_____

How does this passage apply to your purpose?

_____

_____

_____

_____

_____

_____

_____

_____

How often do you go to God for instruction regarding what to do in a given situation?

_____

_____

_____

_____

_____

_____

_____

What does your prayer life look like? How could you improve in this area?

_____

_____

_____

_____

_____

_____

_____

Do you think our destiny is inevitable? Why or why not?

_____

_____

_____

_____

_____

_____

Which of the verses written by Paul at the end of this chapter stands out to you? What do the verses have in common?

_____

_____

_____

_____

_____

_____

_____

_____

_____

_____

Are you ready to be sent by the Lord? What is inhibiting you from submitting fully to His plan?

_____

_____

_____

_____

_____

_____

_____

_____

_____

_____

_____

CHAPTER 3

MARCHING ORDERS

Understand that the call and marching orders from the very plan and purpose of God are the foundation of qualification.

REVIEW, REFLECT, AND RESPOND

> *So Jesus said to them again,*
> *"Peace be with you; as the Father*
> *has sent Me, I also send you.*
>
> *—John 20:21*

Consider the scripture above and answer the following questions:

What did Jesus mean when He said the Father sent Him?

_____

_____

_____

_____

_____

_____

What did and does Jesus mean by, "I also send you"? Is this the same sending the Father did to Jesus Christ?

_____

_____

_____

_____

_____

_____

_____

What are we commissioned by Jesus Christ to do?

_____

_____

_____

_____

_____

_____

_____

How can we be qualified to carry out the commission of Christ?

_____

_____

_____

_____

_____

_____

_____

What is the significance of the order of what Jesus said in Matthew 4:19-20? What does this reveal?

_____

_____

_____

_____

_____

_____

What marching orders have you received from God recently?

_____

_____

_____

_____

_____

_____

Have you ever received marching orders from God that seemed impossible to accomplish? What happened?

_____

_____

_____

_____

_____

_____

_____

Do you trust God to supply you with what you need to fulfill the purpose He has placed on your life? Why or why not?

_____

_____

_____

_____

_____

_____

How did Jesus respond to God the Father when He was sent? Can you respond in the same way?

_____

_____

_____

_____

_____

_____

_____

_____

Where do you go for information besides God? Whom do you allow to speak into your life?

_____

_____

_____

_____

_____

_____

_____

_____

When your back is to the wall, and you don't know what to do, how do you respond? Be honest. Do you believe this is how God wants you to respond?

_____

_____

_____

_____

_____

_____

_____

_____

_____

What does it mean to submit to being sent? Have you done this?

_____

_____

_____

_____

_____

_____

_____

_____

TO WHAT OR TO WHOM ARE YOU SUBMITTING YOUR LIFE?

Often, people think they are just not going to decide anything at all and instead choose to revert to some kind of passive mode. In reality, they have already made a decision to let circumstance determine the outcome.

REVIEW, REFLECT, AND RESPOND

As you read Chapter 4: "To What or to Whom Are You Submitting Your Life?" in *Sent...* review, reflect on, and respond to the text by answering the following questions.

Who is in control of your life—who have you submitted to? Yourself? God? Others?

_____

_____

_____

_____

_____

_____

_____

_____

_____

_____

In what ways are we bonded with Christ? How does this affect our actions?

_____

_____

_____

_____

_____

_____

_____

_____

_____

_____

_____

> *No one can serve two masters; for either he will hate the one and love the other, or he will be devoted to one and despise the other.*
>
> *—Matthew 6:24*

Consider the scripture above and answer the following questions:

What do you think this verse reveals about our obedience to the Lord?

_____

_____

_____

_____

_____

_____

_____

_____

Has a competing "master" ever distracted you from fully submitting and serving God? What was it? What was the outcome?

_____

_____

_____

_____

_____

_____

_____

_____

What worldly "masters" do you despise as a result of your submission to God?

_____

_____

_____

_____

_____

_____

_____

What is a "mindset of purpose"? How can you come to adopt this mindset?

_____

_____

_____

_____

_____

_____

_____

How is a mindset of purpose demonstrated through the life, ministry, and actions of Jesus Christ?

_____

_____

_____

_____

_____

What does an attitude of submission look like in action? Do you operate with an attitude of submission?

_____

_____

_____

_____

_____

_____

_____

_____

_____

_____

What does it mean to have an attitude of initiative? How do you know what to do yourself and what to leave to God?

_____

_____

_____

_____

_____

_____

_____

_____

_____

_____

_____

_____

WHOSE PROMOTIONAL PACKAGE ARE YOU UNLOADING?

There is no end to the proclamation of the gospel and kingdom of God, even to this day.

READING TIME

As you read Chapter 5: "Whose Promotional Package Are You Unloading?" in *Sent...* review, reflect on, and respond to the text by answering the following questions.

REVIEW, REFLECT, AND RESPOND

What avenues can be used to share the gospel of Jesus Christ? Can you foresee any new avenues being added to this list in the near future?

_____

_____

_____

_____

_____

_____

_____

_____

_____

_____

_____

_____

_____

_____

_____

_____

_____

_____

_____

_____

Consider the scripture above and answer the following questions:

How can you discern between those who are actually sheep and those that are ravenous wolves?

_____

_____

_____

_____

_____

_____

_____

_____

Have you ever caught yourself listening to the empty words of a ravenous wolf? What did you realize?

_____

_____

_____

_____

_____

_____

_____

_____

What and whom are you promoting through your life?

_____

_____

_____

_____

_____

_____

What message did Jesus Christ portray through His life?

_____

_____

_____

_____

_____

_____

_____

Why do you live the way you do—what is your motivation? What was Jesus's motivation?

_____

_____

_____

_____

_____

_____

_____

What stands out to you from what the Pharisees and Sadducees did wrong throughout this chapter? Have you ever been guilty of something similar?

_____

_____

_____

_____

_____

_____

_____

_____

_____

What does it mean to deny yourself? Is this a one-time decision or an ongoing process?

_____

_____

_____

_____

_____

_____

_____

_____

_____

_____

What promotional package are you unloading? Does this need to change?

_____

_____

_____

_____

_____

_____

_____

_____

_____

_____

_____

_____

EXCLUSIVE RIGHTS

Jesus was the One who extended the exclusive rights to us.

REVIEW, REFLECT, AND RESPOND

As you read
Chapter 6:
"Exclusive
Rights" in
Sent... review,
reflect on,
and respond
to the text by
answering
the following
questions.

What exclusive rights do you have through
Jesus Christ?

_____

_____

_____

_____

_____

_____

_____

_____

_____

_____

How often do you utilize these exclusive
rights?

_____

_____

_____

_____

_____

_____

_____

_____

_____

_____

_____

_____

> *And we know that God causes all things to work together for good to those who love God, to those who are called according to His purpose. For those whom He foreknew, He also predestined to become conformed to the image of His Son, so that He would be the firstborn among many brothers and sisters; and these whom He predestined, He also called; and these whom He called, He also justified; and these whom He justified, He also glorified.*
>
> *—Romans 8:28-30*

Consider the scripture above and answer the following questions:

What stands out to you from this passage?

_____

_____

_____

_____

_____

_____

_____

What does it mean to be "called according to His purpose"?

_____

_____

_____

_____

_____

_____

_____

What is the only way we can become fruitful? Explain.

_____

_____

_____

_____

_____

_____

_____

_____

_____

_____

How does the Holy Spirit assist us? How attentive are you to the voice of the Holy Spirit?

_____

_____

_____

_____

_____

_____

_____

_____

_____

_____

_____

What is the significance of Jesus being in the Father and us being in Jesus?

_____

_____

_____

_____

_____

_____

_____

_____

What determines our legacy? What will your legacy be by these standards?

_____

_____

_____

_____

_____

_____

_____

_____

Printed in the USA
CPSIA information can be obtained
at www.ICGtesting.com
JSHW010515110124
55119JS00010B/173